MEET GEORGE GERSHWIN AT THE KEYBOARD

16 SONG HITS ARRANGED BY THE COMPOSER

THE CHAPPELL AUTHENTIC

EDITION

© 2006 by Faber Music Ltd
First published by International Music Publications Ltd
International Music Publications Ltd is a Faber Music company
Bloomsbury House 74–77 Great Russell Street London WC1B 3DA
Printed in England by Caligraving Ltd
All rights reserved

ISBN10: 0-571-52677-2
EAN13: 978-0-571-52677-2

To buy Faber Music publications or to find out about the full range of titles available,
please contact your local music retailer or Faber Music sales enquiries:

Faber Music Ltd, Burnt Mill, Elizabeth Way, Harlow, CM20 2HX England
Tel: +44(0)1279 82 89 82   Fax: +44(0)1279 82 89 83
sales@fabermusic.com   fabermusic.com

ABOUT THE GERSHWINS

Among the successful song-writing teams on the musical scene, and there have been many, a very special niche will always be reserved for the amazing Gershwin brothers: Ira, one of the truly outstanding lyricists of our times and George, the transcendent, who encompassed both the popular and serious fields of music.

The first and second of four children born to Morris and Rose Bruskin Gershwin, when viewed almost two decades after the untimely passing of the younger, have taken on qualities of musical stability beyond even the predictions made during their hey-day as co-writers. George was called a "jazz composer" during the 20's and 30's, and we now see that although his work does still fit that classification he was much more. His voice in American Music, with a strong assist from Ira's lyrics, comes closest to the universal. Every facet of the musical scene now reflects the light of their efforts: the jazz combos seemingly never tire of improvising on their great tunes, nor do the popular singers, the torch singers, the serious recitalists, the symphony orchestras, the dance bands, the school orchestras, the choruses and bands, the ballet and the opera—and happily, this is true the world over.

Their father was a man of many ventures who moved his family frequently through various neighborhoods of New York City. Meanwhile, Arthur and Frances joined the family as the third and fourth children. Ira attended Public School No. 20 at Rivington and Forsyth Streets, and when he was fourteen it was decided to add a piano to the family possessions upon which it was intended that he should commence study.

As soon as the piano was put into position in the living room, George promptly sat down and played one of the popular songs of the day. Unknown to his family he had inveigled the use of a friend's pianola and had by himself arrived at a few basic musical concepts. Even so, it was Ira who started lessons. His teacher was also his aunt, and although he showed a genuine musical sensitivity his progress was sluggish and it was decided he could bow out in favour of George.

Miss Green, George's first teacher, soon proved inadequate, as did other neighbourhood teachers, including a Mr. Goldfarb who was the leader of a Hungarian Band. George's first genuinely professional training came from Charles Hambitzer.

According to David Ewen, "Hambitzer later said that what attracted him immediately to Gershwin was the boy's deadly seriousness. Hambitzer offered to teach the boy, refusing to accept any payment for lessons. He became the most important single influence in Gershwin's musical development, probably the decisive influence."*
* A Journey To Greatness, Henry Holt, 1956.

George went on to the High School of Commerce while Ira prepared for college. Ira was an avid reader, especially of light verse; he also preferred dime novels to piano lessons. He was art editor of his high school newspaper and later, at C.C.N.Y., he was a regular contributor to various college periodicals. Ira and college studies were not especially compatible, and although the magazine "Smart Set" (published by H.L.Mencken and George Jean Nathan) accepted a piece of his, it wasn't long before he rather impulsively took a job with Col. Lagg's Greater Empire Shows, a travelling carnival. He worked for five months as cashier and then returned to New York to continue experiments as a lyricist.

Meantime George had been trying his hand at writing popular songs and had decided that the only practical way to advance himself was to enter Tin Pan Alley. He persuaded his mother that he should quit school, at the age of fifteen, to take a job as song plugger and staff pianist at the Jerome H. Remick Company.

The hours were long and arduous, pounding out Remick's roster of "plug tunes" for vaudevillians and singing artists of the day. These people came to the publisher's offices to audition, select and rehearse new material for their acts. There were times when George was sent out to cafes, restaurants, or music stores to play Remick songs or accompany singers in them. It wasn't long before the work became drudgery. Even so, George stuck it out for over two years and always referred to it as very valuable experience. He learned all the tricks of the current composers, but their endless musical clichés exhausted him. He longed for imaginative writing and for original expression. He himself wrote profusely during this period. An admirer of the work of Irving Berlin and Jerome Kern, George was also much influenced by the rag-time and jazz of the day.

He tried to get his own songs published, both at Remick and at other publishers, without avail. In 1916 Harry Von Tilzer accepted "When You Want 'Em You Can't Get 'Em," for which George received five dollars. The lyricist, Murray Roth, was more persuasive and got fifteen. However, George was proud; it was his first song in print.

He and Roth were able to audition another song they had written for the Shubert office. Although nothing happened directly, it did lead George to a contact with Sigmund Romberg, then chief composer for the Shuberts. His second song for publication was a little two-four number, "Making of a Girl," written with Romberg and Harold Atteridge and used in "The Passing Show of 1916." Then early in 1917 Remick accepted a rag-time instrumental entitled "Rialto Ripples" written with Will Donaldson.

At this stage George became rehearsal pianist for the Dillingham-Ziegfeld production "Miss 1917," with music by Victor Herbert and Jerome Kern. Miss Vivienne Segal, starring in the show, introduced two of George's numbers at one of the regular Sunday night concerts given at the Century Theatre. George had also served as accompanist for these concerts and had deeply impressed the company with his talents. Harry Askin, the company manager, later was instrumental in bringing him to the attention of Max Dreyfus, the publisher.

Dreyfus signed George to a contract, at thirty-five dollars a week, to do no more than just keep writing. During this period many of George's songs were interpolated into various Broadway shows. His reputation in the trade was growing rapidly, and although he still had not been fortunate enough to click with a smash hit, his position was becoming established in spite of his tender years. He continued with his studies and attended recitals and concerts as often as possible. Most of his songs at that time were written with Irving Caesar doing the lyrics.

Ira had been working at odd jobs since returning from his fling with the carnival. He began collaborating with George on some of these interpolated songs. Not wishing to be accused of basking in George's new glory, Ira used the pseudonym Arthur Francis (concocted from the names of his other brother and his sister). Their first joint effort was called "The Real American Folk Song" and was sung by Nora Bayes in the show, "Ladies First," but was never published.

Ira's first published song was "Waiting For The Sun," written with George and used in "The Sweetheart Shop." Ira continued the use of his penname until 3 years after he had completed the lyrics for the production "Two Little Girls In Blue" with Vincent Youmans and Paul Lannin doing the music. He later resumed his own name professionally and continued to work with George and also with Lewis Gensler, Milton Schwartzwald, Joseph Meyer, Philip Charig, Lou Silvers and others.

George's first chance to be the main composer for a show had come in 1918. At least one resounding fiasco is probably a good experience for every young composer, and George got his out of his system before he was twenty. "Half Past Eight" looked like a good idea on paper, but after one wild week of production in Syracuse George was lucky to have train fare back to New York. But with his customary resiliency he bounced right back.

A young producer, Alex Aarons, entered the picture in 1919 and commissioned George to compose the score for "La La Lucille." Aarons himself was a musician, and his faith in George was well placed. The show enjoyed a strong run, until the Actors' strike in 1919 closed the theatres of New York. The same year he and Irving Caesar had their song "Swanee" introduced at the Capitol Theatre, and the following year when Al Jolson used it in his show "Sinbad" it really caught on. George had his first smash hit before his 21st birthday.

In the memorial volume, "George Gershwin," edited by Merle Armitage, Ira has described the next few very important years in George's life.

Beginning in 1920 he wrote, among other things, the music for "George White's Scandals" for five consecutive years. It was for the fourth of this series that he and B. G. DeSylva turned out in six days a short one-act

opera called "135th Street." Lasting only one night it was eliminated not because it was ineffective artistically but because it changed the mood of the audience and the tragic note it injected in the proceedings handicapped the gayer numbers that followed. Intimations of the musical paths George was later to follow, especially in recitative, may be found in "135th Street." It was also in 1923 that Eva Gauthier, with George at the piano, introduced a group of popular and musical comedy songs at an Aeolian Hall recital. It included numbers by George, Kern, Berlin and Donaldson. Needless to say, this concert caused quite a commotion in musical circles.

Early in 1924, Paul Whiteman announced a concert with new works by Deems Taylor, Victor Herbert and George Gershwin. The newspaper item was the first inkling George had that Whiteman was serious when he had once casually mentioned that some day he expected to do such a concert and hoped for a contribution from George. George decided to chance it. Three weeks later, with an orchestration by Ferde Grofé, Whiteman was rehearsing "Rhapsody In Blue" in the night club, Palais Royal. A week later when it was presented at Aeolian Hall with the composer at the piano, the response was immediate. Soon it was being played all over the world.

A year after the 'Rhapsody' appeared Walter Damrosch commissioned George to compose a work of symphonic scope for the New York Symphony Society. The 'Concerto In F' resulted. Incidentally, this was the first time my brother did his own orchestration; all he had ever done in this line was a number or two in "Primrose," an operetta he wrote in London. To do the scoring of the 'Concerto' George rented a couple of rooms at a hotel in order to have comparative quiet from the noisy and busy private house we lived in with the rest of the family. In those two small hotel rooms, within a period of less than three months, he not only orchestrated this work but worked with me on "Tip-Toes" and at the same time collaborated with Herbert Stothart on "Song of the Flame." All three works had their premieres within a few days of each other and in addition, Whiteman revived '135th Street' in a concert at Carnegie Hall. With George playing six performances of the 'Concerto' during that period under Damrosch in New York, Philadelphia and Baltimore, his energy was seemingly inexhaustible. As he had a very special affection for the 'Concerto' it is interesting to note, even if one doesn't believe in artistic yardsticks, that in 1930 when Albert Coates, the eminent English conductor, compiled a list of "Fifty Best Works in Music" there was included only one American work and that was the 'Concerto in F.'"

In 1924 the fabulous parade of hit shows began for George and Ira working both together and separately. For the producing firm of Aarons and Freedley the brothers contributed the music and lyrics to "Lady, Be Good!," "Tip-Toes," "Oh, Kay!," "Funny Face," "Treasure Girl," "Girl Crazy," and "Pardon My English."

4

With George S. Kaufman and Morrie Ryskind they created "Strike Up The Band," "Of Thee I Sing" (Pulitzer prize of 1932) and "Let 'Em Eat Cake." For ten years song hit after song hit swept the country. "Fascinating Rhythm," "The Man I Love," "Oh, Lady Be Good!," "Clap Yo' Hands," "Do-Do-Do," "Love Is Sweeping the Country," "Someone To Watch Over Me," "'S Wonderful," "Soon," "I've Got A Crush On You," "Liza," "Embraceable You" and "I Got Rhythm," to name just a few.

Ira, working with other composers, also chalked up an impressive list that included "Sunny Disposish," "Cheerful Little Earful," "Fun To Be Fooled," "Let's Take A Walk Around The Block," and "You're A Builder Upper."

In 1923 George had made the first five trips he was to take across the Atlantic, mostly to do shows such as the rollicking success "Primrose" in London. These trips culminated in his memorable visit to Paris in the spring of 1928 during which he conceived much of "An American in Paris." On December 13, 1928, with Walter Damrosch conducting the Philharmonic-Symphony Society of New York, "An American in Paris" received its premiere in Carnegie Hall. The work has since taken its regular place in the repertoire of symphony orchestras all over the world.

Travelling and serious writing seemed to dovetail quite comfortably for George. In the winter of 1930 he and Ira went to Hollywood to work on the film "Delicious." What was born of a short orchestral sequence for the picture and called "Rhapsody In Rivets" became the "Second Rhapsody" for piano and orchestra. Isaac Goldberg, his biographer, quotes George with reference to the work, "I wrote it mainly because I wanted to write a serious composition and found the opportunity in California to do it. Nearly everybody comes back from California with a western tan and a pocketful of moving picture money. I decided to come back with both those things, and a serious composition—if the climate would let me. I was under no obligation to the picture company to do this. But, you know, the old artistic soul must every so often be appeased."

In fact, as George's renown increased so did his travels. Appearances as soloist and conductor were numerous and widespread throughout the country. On one of his trips to Cuba he was inspired to write "Rumba" (later called "Cuban Overture"). This work was introduced at one of his appearances at Lewisohn Stadium, August 16, 1932.

The Stadium Concerts "All Gershwin" programmes have a regular feature every summer in New York City. These programmes have been held annually since the days when George was a regular participant and continue to be sellout events every year. Since his death the number of "Gershwin Memorial" concerts elsewhere in the world is beyond tabulation.

Much has been written about George and his temperament. His character has been painted frequently in rather bright colours. Could it be that many of his friends, being rather colourful writers and living during a rather colourful period, have given a somewhat heightened and exaggerated view of his personality? His intimates who were professionals in the music field rather than professional personalities picture a different man.

Paul Whiteman has said, "George Gershwin was a sweet person and a wonderful character,—logically naive throughout his short life and apparently unaware of his genius." It is obvious that there was a strong quality of musical integrity in him; his continuous study of music throughout his life is indicative of this. After his years with Charles Hambitzer he studied theory and composition with the eminent teacher Edward Kilenyi and still later did advanced study with Joseph Schillinger.

When Hambitzer brought George to Kilenyi he said of him, "The Boy is not only talented but is uncommonly serious in his search for knowledge of music." Later Kilenyi expressed his feelings. "When he talked he was soft-spoken. Whatever I showed him he assimilated and used to advantage."

In 1937, having written his opera and seen it most successfully performed, George was with Ira in Hollywood working on a series of pictures when he developed the severe headaches that later proved to have been caused by a brain tumor. He died Sunday morning, July 11, 1937, in Los Angeles, at the age of 38.

Ira went into temporary retirement at this point but, happily for us, has since resumed his co-writing efforts with a variety of composers. With George he had written the lyrics for eighteen productions in addition to their film scores.

In temperament and personality the two were direct opposites. Younger brother George was moody, given to hours of solitude, careless of health and nerves, and would flash with ideas on the spur of the moment. Ira is patient, careful in his research, painstaking with every word, but withal a colourful lyric-writer, a sounder of ringing syllables. With all the differences in temperament, there was an essential alikeness between the brothers, not alone of blood, but in approach to people and to life. Rather than argue, they would change a word, a note. Rather than offend, they would agree with the director, singer or artist, and work out a compromise.

Ira is thoughtful, generous, friendly in his personal dealings, easy to get along with and to talk to, and yet is no star-gazer. He is little given to effusiveness. In his own field he has rigid ideas of behaviour and is quick with the fast quip at the ego-stretched genius or the frenzied temperamental whose every line is God-given and sacred. He thinks success is not success if it affects personal attitudes and has no patience with the several "greatest living songwriters" who absorb their own publicity, devour handy compliments, and purr under back pats.

Of brother George, Ira has said, "Despite his apparent egocentricity (to some), he was actually quite modest about his talent and accomplishments."

THE MAN I LOVE

Music and Lyrics by GEORGE GERSHWIN and IRA GERSHWIN

5

Slow and in singing style

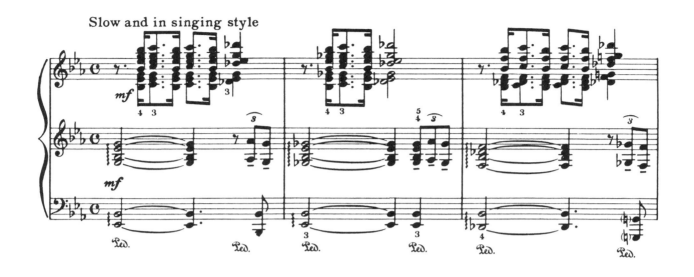

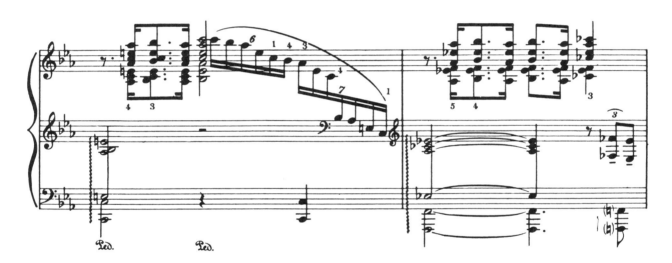

46086

I'LL BUILD A STAIRWAY TO PARADISE

Music and Lyrics by GEORGE GERSHWIN, B. G. DE SYLVA and ARTHUR FRANCIS

Vigorously

DO IT AGAIN

Music and Lyrics by GEORGE GERSHWIN and B. G. DE SYLVA

FASCINATING RHYTHM

Music and Lyrics by GEORGE GERSHWIN and IRA GERSHWIN

46086

OH, LADY BE GOOD

Music and Lyrics by GEORGE GERSHWIN and IRA GERSHWIN

Rather slow (with humour)

il basso marcato

poco a poco cresc.

SOMEBODY LOVES ME

Music and Lyrics by GEORGE GERSHWIN, B. G. DE SYLVA and BALLARD MACDONALD

SWEET AND LOW DOWN

Music and Lyrics by GEORGE GERSHWIN and IRA GERSHWIN

CLAP YO' HANDS

Music and Lyrics by GEORGE GERSHWIN and IRA GERSHWIN

GEORGE and IRA GERSHWIN

DO DO DO

Music and Lyrics by GEORGE GERSHWIN and IRA GERSHWIN

MY ONE AND ONLY

Music and Lyrics by GEORGE GERSHWIN and IRA GERSHWIN

'S WONDERFUL

Music and Lyrics by GEORGE GERSHWIN and IRA GERSHWIN

STRIKE UP THE BAND

Music and Lyrics by GEORGE GERSHWIN and IRA GERSHWIN

I GOT RHYTHM

Music and Lyrics by GEORGE GERSHWIN and IRA GERSHWIN

WHO CARES?

Music and Lyrics by GEORGE GERSHWIN and IRA GERSHWIN

THAT CERTAIN FEELING

Music and Lyrics by GEORGE GERSHWIN and IRA GERSHWIN

LIZA

Music and Lyrics by GEORGE GERSHWIN, IRA GERSHWIN and GUS KAHN